AF605677
N
W
E
S
QLD
QUEENSLAND
SA
SOUTH AUSTRALIA
NSW
NEW SOUTH WALES
ACT
AUSTRALIAN CAPITAL TERRITORY
VIC
VICTORIA
TAS
TASMANIA

KYLE SURRY
KIDS' GUIDE TO AUSTRALIA'S STATES & TERRITORIES
DISCOVERING
VIC
VICTORIA
REDBACK publishing

First Published 2026 by
Redback Publishing
Suite 6, 13a Narabang Way,
Belrose NSW 2085
Australia

www.redbackpublishing.com
orders@redbackpublishing.com

ISBN 978-1-761400-66-7

Author: Kyle Surry
Editors: Lucinda Dodds and Emma Dobinson
Designer: Redback Publishing

Original illustrations © Redback Publishing 2026
Originated by Redback Publishing

Acknowledgements
Abbreviations: l—left, r—right, b—bottom, t—top, c—centre, m—middle
We would like to thank the following for permission to reproduce photographs: (Images © shutterstock, Alamy) p6 - hwmobs via Flickr, p9br - Unknown author - http://sinpic.slv.vic.gov.au/cgi-bin/Pwebrecon.cgi?DB=local&BBID=49297 [dead link]http://search.slv.vic.gov.au/MAIN:Everything:SLV_VOYAGER1690285, Public Domain, https://commons.wikimedia.org/w/index.php?curid=15058593, p10-11 - John Black Henderson (1827-1918) - State Library of New South Wales, SSV2B/Ball/7, Public Domain, https://commons.wikimedia.org/w/index.php?curid=27221126, p14-15, p20-21, p25br - Paul Harding 00 / Shutterstock.com, p17tmr - Ikonya / Shutterstock.com, p26-27 - Tom Roberts - Parliament of Australia, Public Domain, https://commons.wikimedia.org/w/index.php?curid=1021043, p29ml - Squiresy92 including elements from Sodacan - Own work, CC BY-SA 4.0, https://commons.wikimedia.org/w/index.php?curid=47741958, p31br - ben bryant / Shutterstock.com

A catalogue record for this book is available from the National Library of Australia

Twelve Apostles

A LONG TIME AGO

Who Was There First?

The ancestors of the Indigenous people of Victoria were living there many thousands of years ago. Scientists have found old campsites in the Grampians region that are at least 20,000 years old.

In the Melbourne area, Indigenous Australians hunted animals for food, caught fish, eels and collected oysters. They also enjoyed many vegetables, nuts, seeds and fruits. Along rivers and valleys there was plenty of food for hunting, fishing and gathering.

Mackenzie Waterfall

The Grampians has the largest number of rock art sites in the southern part of Australia.

Rock art along the Gulgurn Manja Shelter Walk in the Grampians.

COLONY OF VICTORIA

Victoria was originally part of the colony of New South Wales and was known as the Port Phillip District.

In 1851, Victoria became a separate colony with its own government.

Convicts were never sent directly to Port Phillip from England. Most of them were moved there from New South Wales or Van Diemen's Land.

The explorers Bass and Flinders proved that Victoria was not connected to Tasmania when they sailed through Bass Strait in 1798, ten years after the first British settlement in Australia.

Melbourne

In 1835, John Batman chose the site for a settlement which was later called the Port Phillip District. This is now Melbourne and its suburbs.

GOLD RUSH

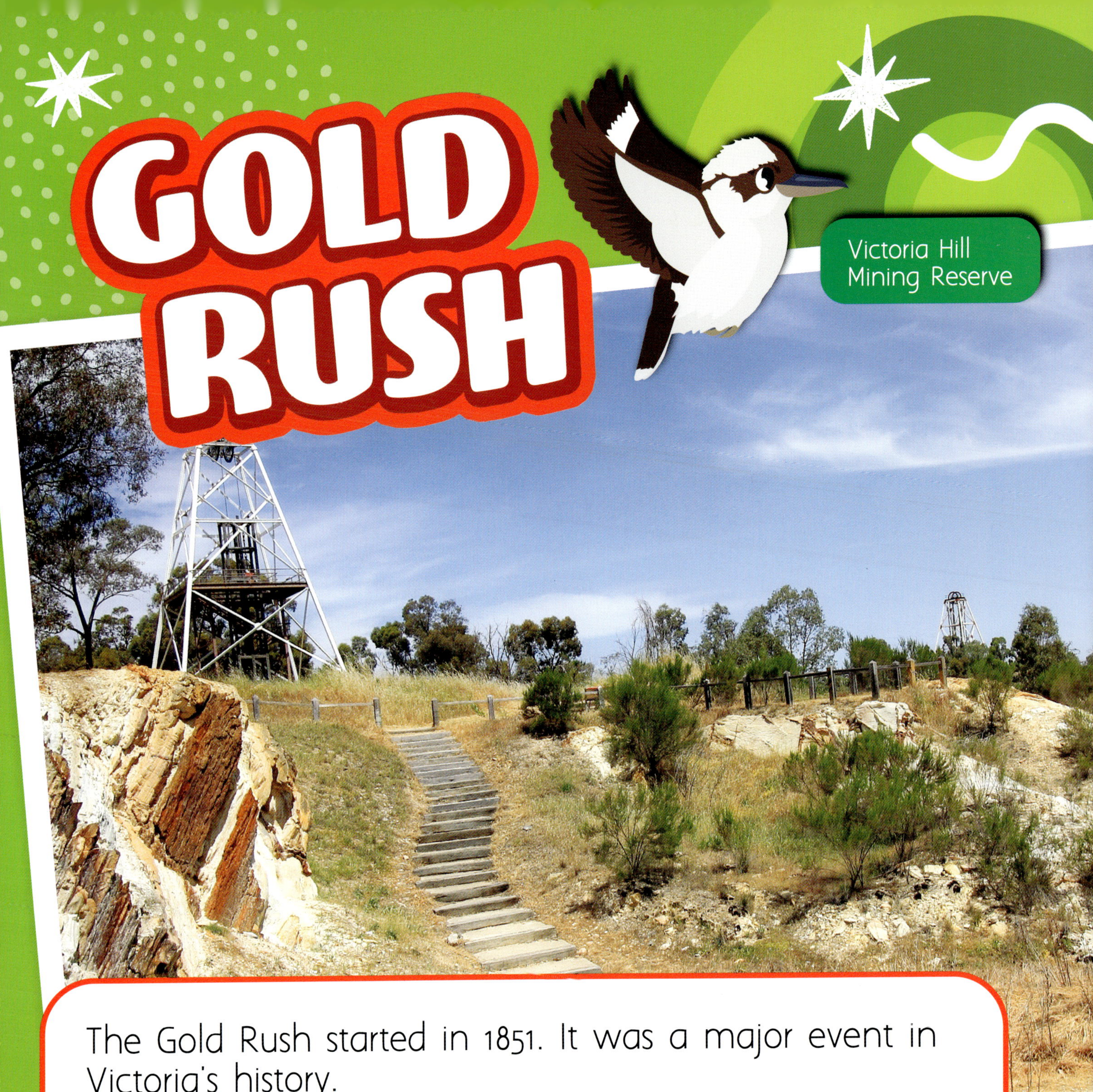

The Gold Rush started in 1851. It was a major event in Victoria's history.

People came from around the world to look for gold. The wealth created by gold mining turned small country villages into large towns with many buildings.

Hundreds of tonnes of gold were mined during the Gold Rush in Victoria.

Victoria's Biggest Gold Mining Towns

- Ararat
- Ballarat
- Bendigo
- Castlemaine

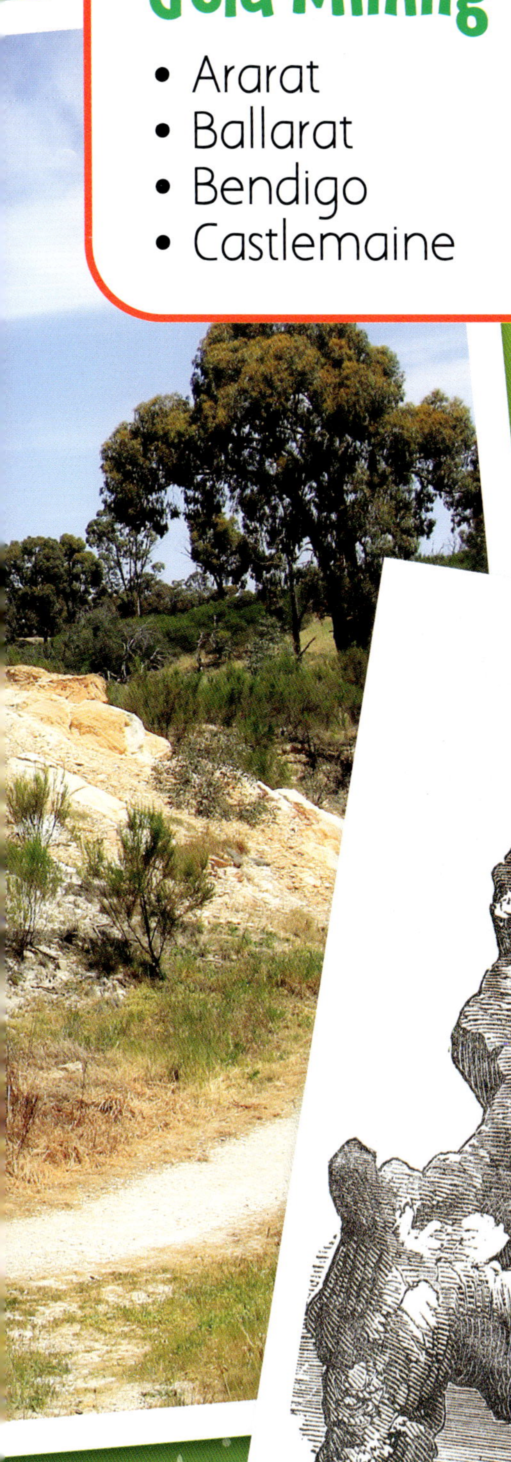

In the ten years after 1851, Victoria produced one third of the world's gold.

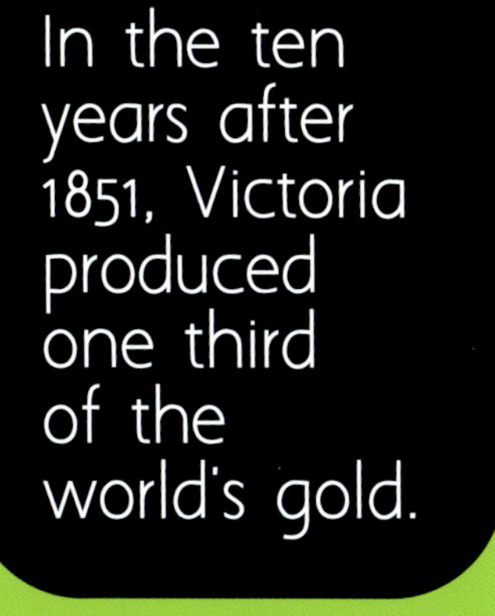

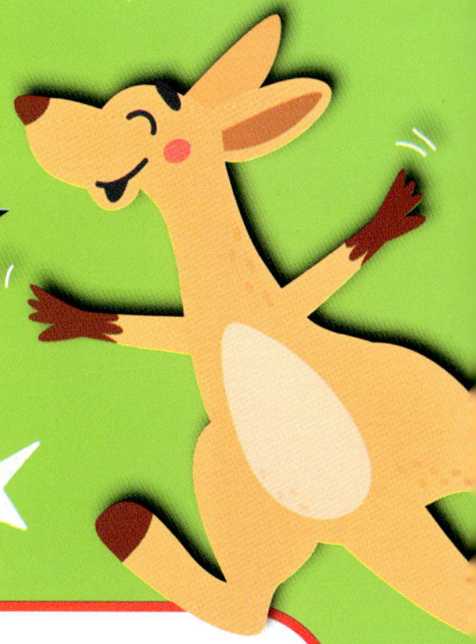

The largest gold nugget found in Victoria weighed as much as a man. It was discovered near Ballarat in 1869 and was called the *Welcome Stranger*.

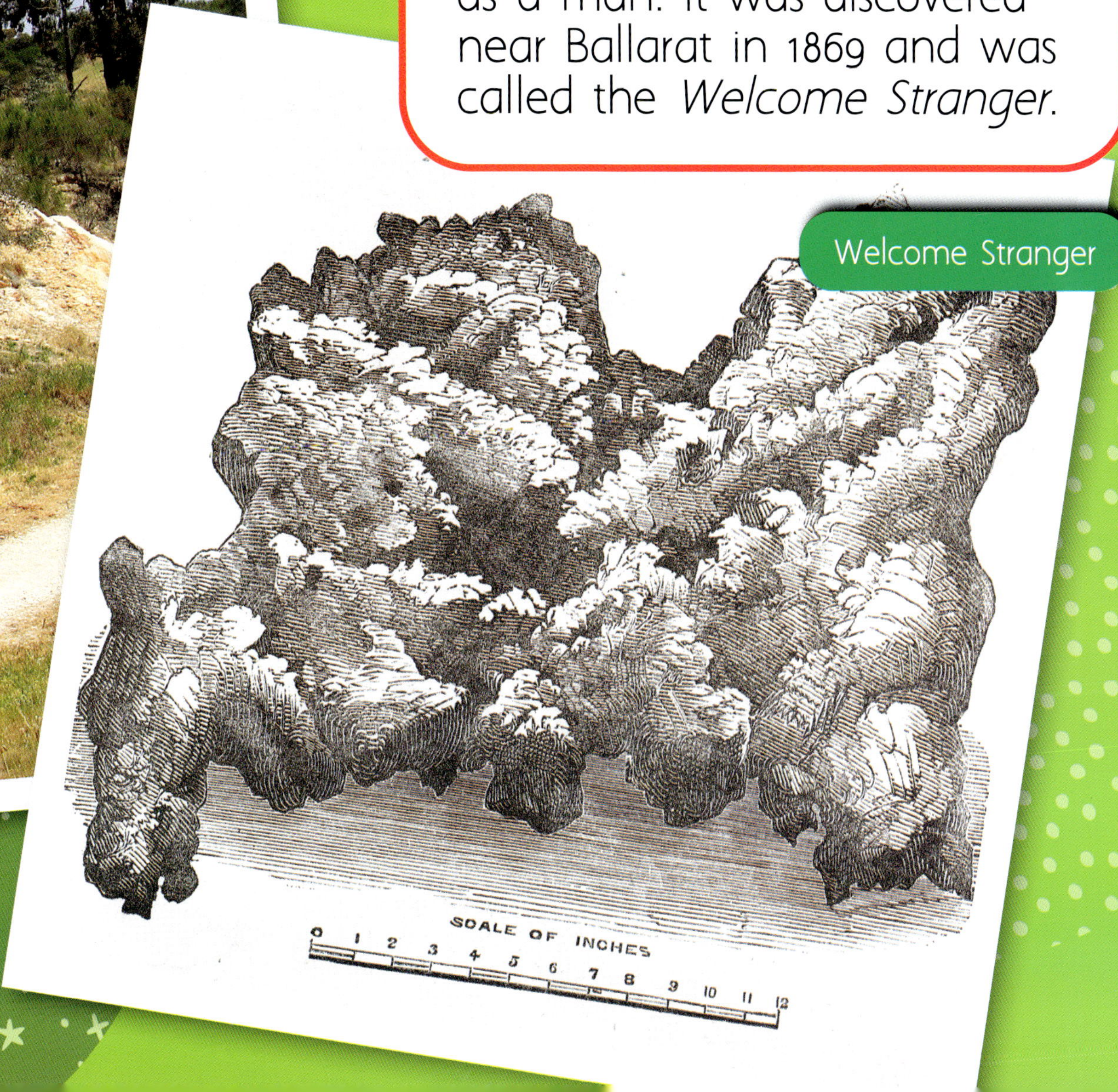

Welcome Stranger

In 1854, goldminers in Ballarat were angry at the high fees they had to pay the government before they were allowed to look for gold.

The protesting miners built a wooden stockade (or fence) around themselves. They then had a fight with soldiers and police. Many people on both sides died.

Eureka flag

The goldminers' Eureka flag has become a well-known symbol all around Australia.

WHERE IS VICTORIA?

Victoria is the second smallest state of Australia, but it has the second largest state population. The capital city is Melbourne on the Yarra River. The state of Victoria was named after Queen Victoria.

Where are the borders of Victoria?

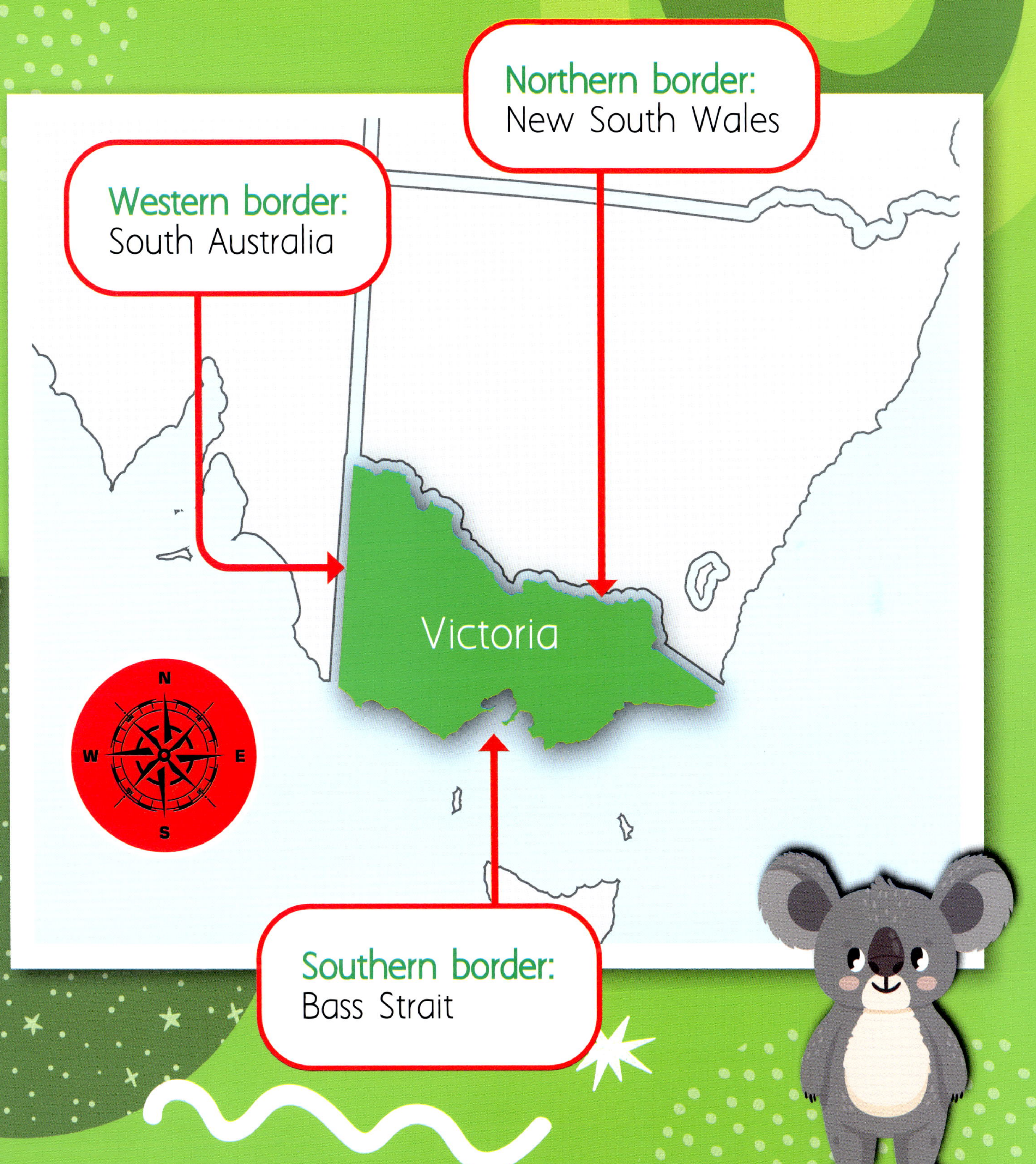

HOW MANY PEOPLE?

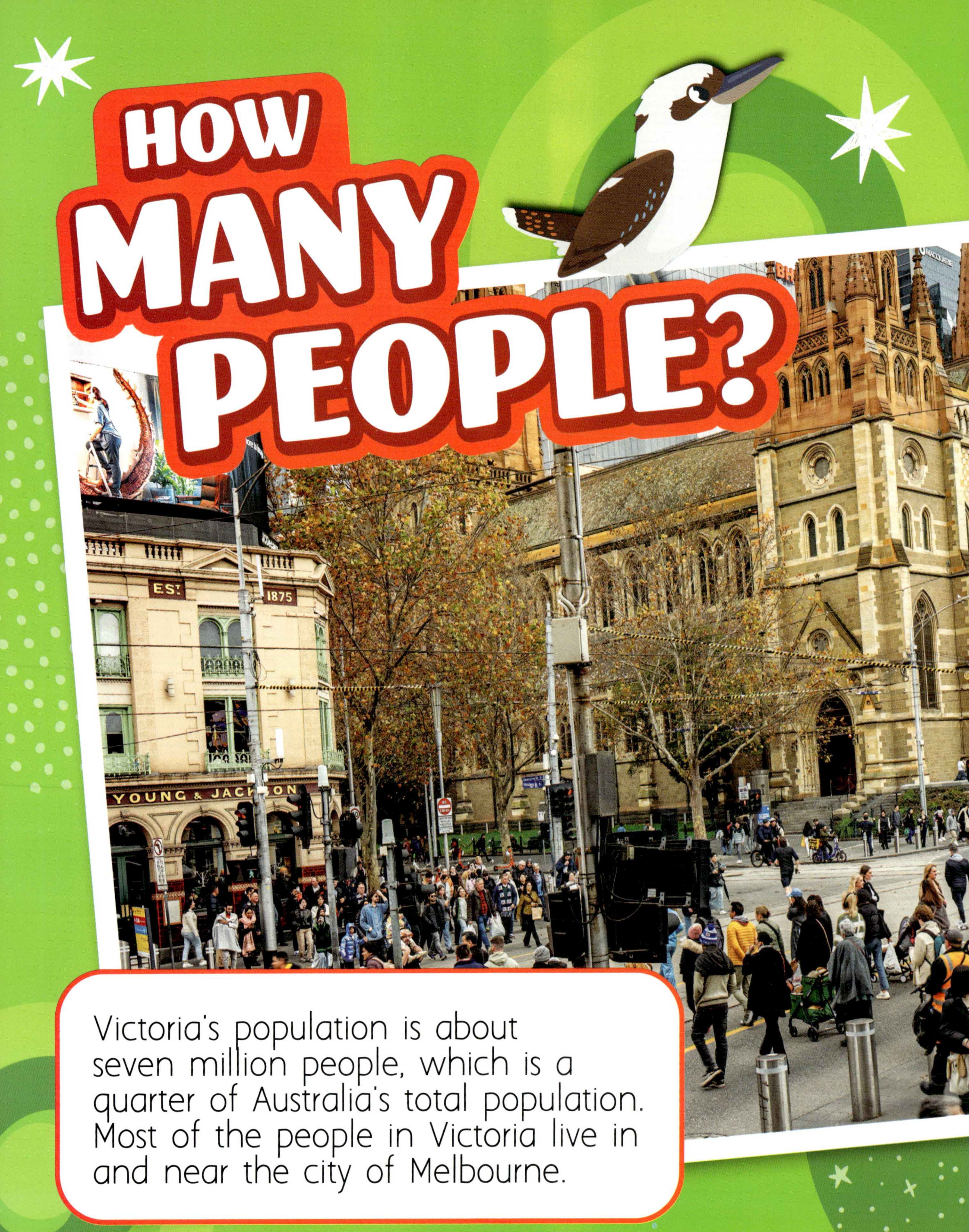

Victoria's population is about seven million people, which is a quarter of Australia's total population. Most of the people in Victoria live in and near the city of Melbourne.

One third of the people in Victoria were born overseas. The top overseas countries of birth were:
• India
• England
• China
• New Zealand
(ABS 2021)
Born in Australia
Born overseas
Nearly four out of every ten people in Victoria say they have no religion.

THE BIGGEST CITIES

Melbourne

Capital city of Victoria, located on Port Phillip Bay and the Yarra River.

Geelong

A port city located beside Corio Bay on the Barwon River.

Ballarat

The place in Victoria where the Gold Rush started in 1851.

Shepparton

Centre of the surrounding agricultural and manufacturing regions.

Bendigo

One of the Gold Rush towns of the 1850s.

Mildura

Located on the Murray River in the north of Victoria.

THE LAND IN VICTORIA

Murray Basin Plains

The Murray Basin Plains are in the north of Victoria and are important for wheat growing. They include the driest parts of Victoria.

Southern Uplands

The Southern Uplands are near the coast south of Melbourne. Wilson's Promontory, which is the most southerly point on the Australian mainland, is in this region.

Southern Plains

The Southern Plains are where Victoria's brown coal deposits are found.

Central Highlands

Mount Bogong is the highest mountain in Victoria. It is part of the Australian Alps.

Phillip Island

Phillip Island is famous for the nightly 'Penguin Parade', when little penguins emerge from the sea and waddle back to their burrows.

Dandenong Ranges

The low hills of the Dandenong Ranges are home to a wide range of wildlife. The area is a popular place for day trips from Melbourne.

PORT PHILLIP BAY

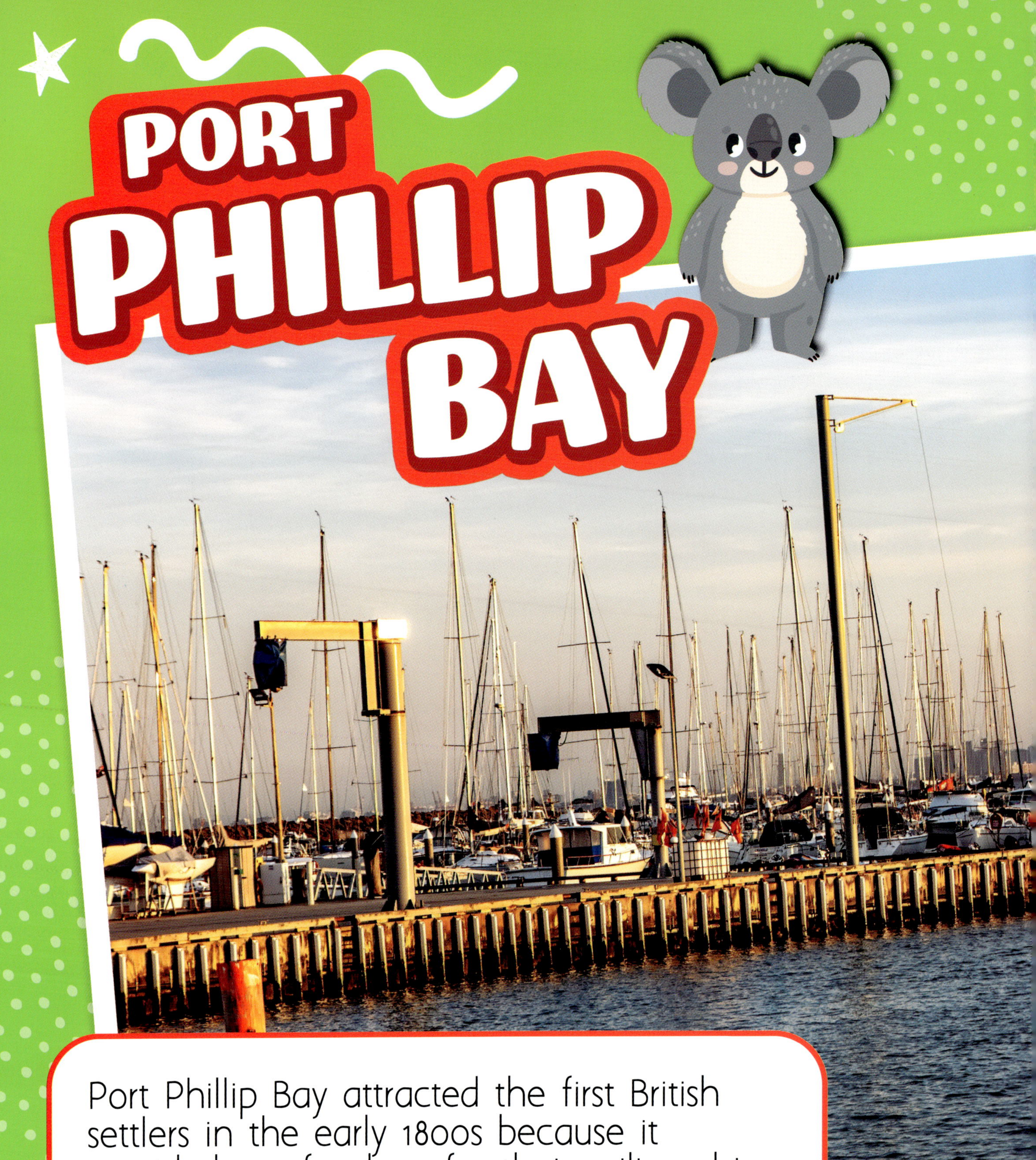

Port Phillip Bay attracted the first British settlers in the early 1800s because it provided a safe place for their sailing ships. Aboriginal people had been living around the bay for thousands of years before then.

Port Phillip Bay is shared by cargo and cruise ships, fishing boats and people enjoying water sports.

In Port Phillip Bay, besides people and their boats, there are also whales, dolphins, birds, fish and may other animals.

Dolphins in Port Phillip Bay

RIVERS IN VICTORIA

Yarra River

The Yarra River flows through Melbourne. Its waters add to Melbourne's water supply. The Wurundjeri name for the river is Birrarung.

The 3 Longest Rivers in Victoria

Murray River

2,530 km long (forms most of Victoria's boundary with NSW)

Goulburn River

583 km long

Glenelg River

454 km long

SPECIAL PLACES IN VICTORIA

Royal Exhibition Building

Built in 1880 for the World's Fair, this is one of the last exhibition style buildings from the 1800s left in the world. Along with its gardens, this building is a World Heritage Site.

Twelve Apostles

These spectacular rock pillars in the sea off the Great Ocean Road are a major tourist attraction.

Great Ocean Road

Follows the coastline from Geelong to the South Australian border and offers wonderful scenery.

Melbourne Cricket Ground (MCG)

The MCG is the largest cricket ground in Australia. In 1956, it was the main centre for the Olympic Games.

GOVERNMENT OF VICTORIA

From the time of the arrival of British settlers, Victoria was a part of New South Wales. In 1851, Victoria became a separate colony. In 1856, the colony of Victoria had its own government. In 1901, Federation meant that the Australian State of Victoria was formed.

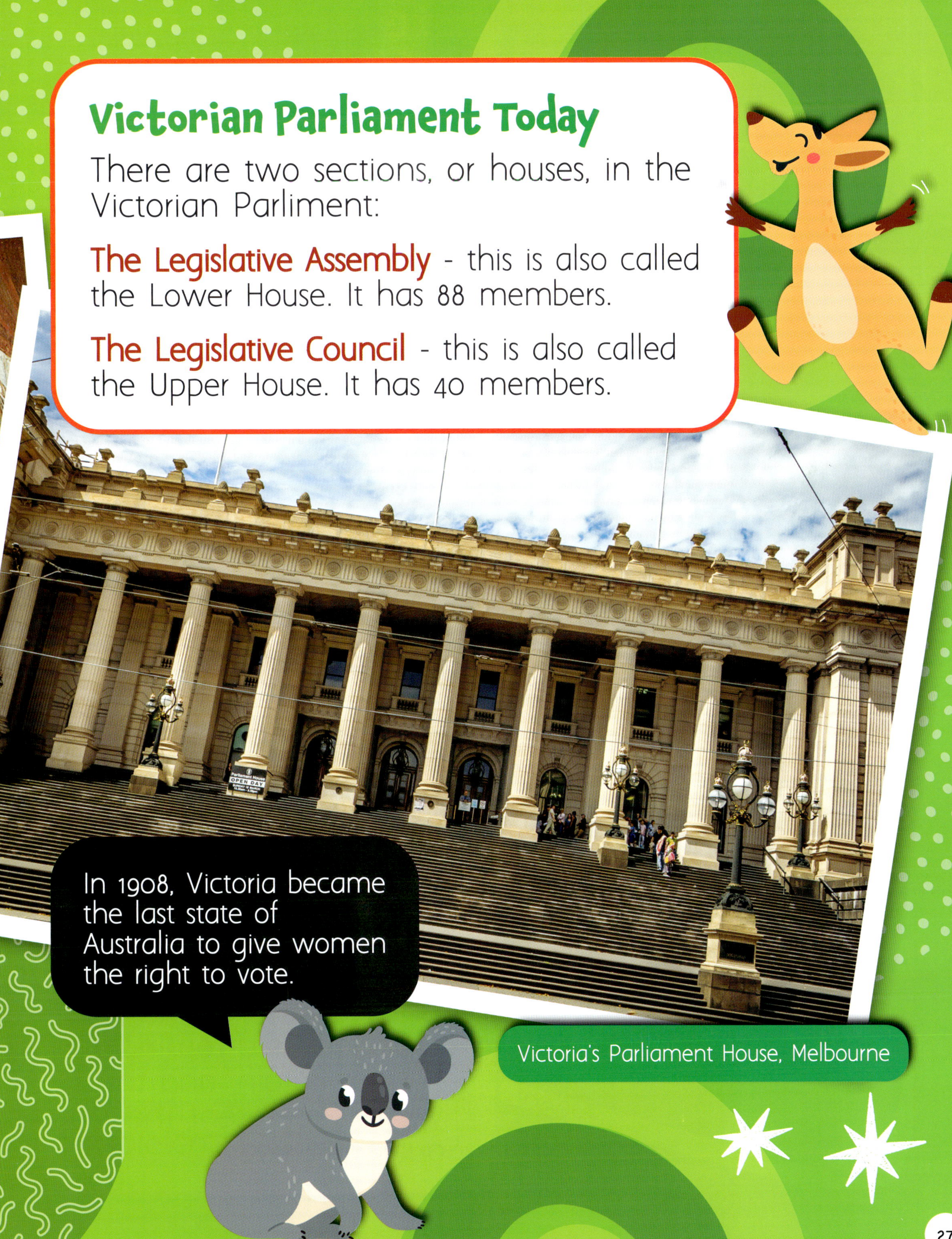

Victorian Parliament Today

There are two sections, or houses, in the Victorian Parliment:

The Legislative Assembly - this is also called the Lower House. It has 88 members.

The Legislative Council - this is also called the Upper House. It has 40 members.

In 1908, Victoria became the last state of Australia to give women the right to vote.

Victoria's Parliament House, Melbourne

MELBOURNE CUP HOLIDAY

Held in Victoria on the first Tuesday in November, this public holiday is for the horse race that is run at Flemington Racecourse. People all around Australia stop whatever they are doing at 3 pm on that day each year to find out which horse will be the winner.

ancestors people from the past who are related to those alive today

colonists people who move to a new country and impose their culture on it

emblem image or design that symbolises something

exhibition big show

nugget small, hard piece of something

stockade fence all around an area

symbol thing or image that represents something else

tonne 1,000 kilograms

World Heritage Site important place listed by the United Nations

Melbourne Central Business District

INDEX

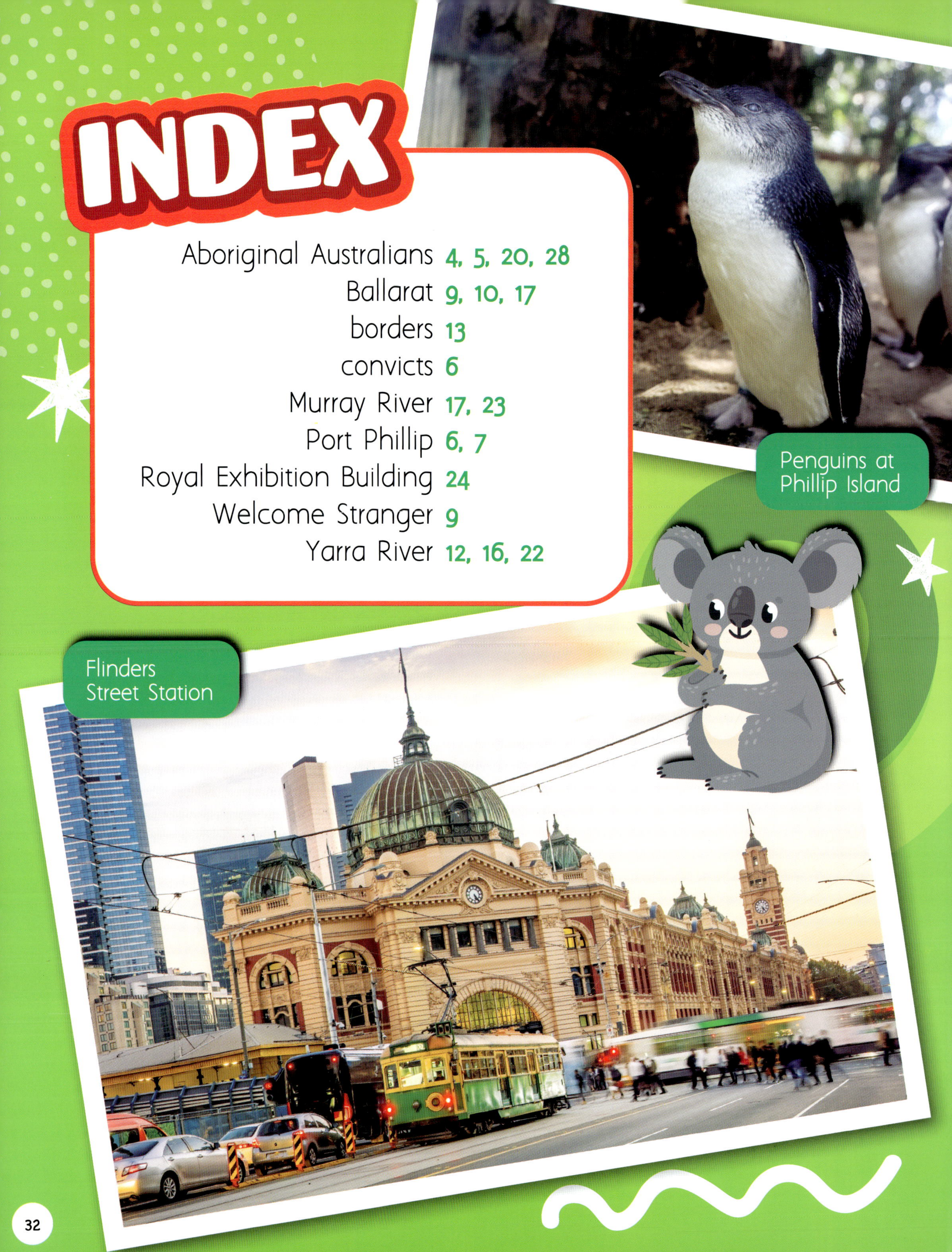

Penguins at Phillip Island

Flinders Street Station

KIDS' GUIDE
TO
AUSTRALIA'S
STATES & TERRITORIES
WA
WESTERN
AUSTRALIA
NT
NORTHERN
TERRITORY